God's Answers to Man's Questions

William MacDonald

God's Answers to Man's Questions
William MacDonald
Published by:
 ECS Ministries
 PO Box 1028
 Dubuque, IA 52004-1028
 phone: (563) 585-2070
 email: ecsorders@ecsministries.org
 website: www.ecsministries.org

First ECS Edition 2012

ISBN 978-1-59387-173-4

Code: W-GAMQ

Copyright © 1958, 2006, 2012 William MacDonald

Previously published by Walterick Publishers © 2006

All rights reserved. No part of this publication may be reproduced or transmitted in any manner, electronic or mechanical, including photocopy, recording, or any information storage and retrieval system including the Internet without written permission from the publisher. Permission is not needed for brief quotations embodied in critical articles and reviews.

All Scripture quotations, unless otherwise indicated, are taken from the New King James Version. Copyright © 1979, 1980, 1982 by Thomas Nelson, Inc. Used by permission. All rights reserved.

Printed in the United States of America

Table of Contents

Let's Get Started 5

The Necessity of Salvation 13

The Work of Christ 16

The Way of Salvation 22

General Difficulties 36

Relationship and Fellowship 40

How to Be Certain of Salvation 46

Holiness 50

"Standing" and "State" 57

After Salvation—What? 60

Let's Get Started

If you want to know what it means to be a follower of Jesus Christ (and how to become one), read on! The Christian message is presented here as a series of questions and answers—the kind of questions you might ask, with answers based directly on the Bible.

Where shall we start?

Let's start with the subject that made the Christian gospel (gospel means "good news") necessary in the first place. That would be the subject of *sin*.

What is sin?

Sin is breaking God's law, that is, doing one's own will without restraint of God or man. It is coming short of God's standard of perfection in thought, word, or deed. It is failure to do what one knows is right. *"For all have sinned and fall short of the glory of God"* (Romans 3:23). *"Therefore, to him who knows to do good and does not do it, to him it is sin"* (James 4:17). *"Whoever commits sin also commits lawlessness, and sin is lawlessness"* (1 John 3:4).

Where did the first sin take place?

The first sin took place in heaven, when Lucifer, the chief of the angels, wanted to take God's place. He was then cast out of heaven and became known as Satan (meaning "adversary"). *"How you are fallen from heaven, O Lucifer, son of the morning! How you are cut down to the ground, you who weakened the nations! For you have said in your heart: 'I will ascend into heaven, I will exalt my throne above the stars of God; I will also sit on the mount of the congregation on the farthest sides of the north; I will ascend above the heights of the clouds, I will be like the Most High.' Yet you shall be brought down to Sheol, to the lowest depths of the Pit"* (Isaiah 14:12-15).

How did sin enter the world?

Sin entered the world through Adam when he disobeyed God by eating of the forbidden fruit in the Garden of Eden. Here is the story as told in the Word of God: *"Now the serpent was more cunning than any beast of the field which the LORD God had made. And he said to the woman, 'Has God indeed said, "You shall not eat of every tree of the garden"?' And the woman said to the serpent, 'We may eat the fruit of the trees of the garden; but of the fruit of the tree which is in the midst of the garden, God has said, "You shall not eat it, nor shall you touch it, lest you die."' Then the serpent said to the woman, 'You will not surely die. For God knows that in the day you eat of it your eyes will be opened, and you will be like God, knowing good and evil.' So when the woman saw that the tree was good for food, that it was pleasant to the eyes, and a tree desirable to make one wise, she took of its fruit and ate. She also gave to her husband with her, and he ate. Then the eyes of both of them were opened, and they knew that they were naked; and they sewed fig leaves together and made themselves coverings. And they heard the sound of the LORD God walking in the garden in the cool of the day, and Adam and his wife hid themselves from the presence of the LORD God among the trees of the garden. Then the LORD God called to Adam and said to him, 'Where are you?' So he said, 'I heard Your voice in the garden, and I was afraid because I was naked; and I hid myself.' And He said, 'Who told you that you were naked? Have you eaten from the tree of which I commanded you that you should not eat?' Then the man said, 'The woman whom You gave to be with me, she gave me of the tree, and I ate.' And the LORD God said to the woman, 'What is this you have done?' The woman said, 'The serpent deceived me, and I ate'"* (Genesis 3:1-13).

Why did God allow sin to enter the world?

God made man as a free, moral agent with the power to choose between good and evil. His desire was that His creatures should choose to love and worship Him voluntarily, and to desire good rather than evil. But if a creature has the power to choose good, he must of necessity also have the power to choose evil. *"Then the LORD God took the man and put him in the garden of Eden to tend and keep it. And the LORD God commanded the man, saying 'Of every tree of the garden you may freely eat; but of the tree of the knowledge of good and evil you shall not eat, for in the day that you eat of it you shall surely die'"* (Genesis 2:15-17).

What would have happened to Adam if he had not sinned?

He would have enjoyed long life in the Garden of Eden (Gen. 2:17).

What happened to Adam when he did sin?

Three things happened immediately to Adam when he sinned.

1. He became spiritually dead toward God.

2. He became subject to physical suffering, sickness, and death.

3. He lost his innocence, became unrighteous and unholy, guilty and lost, an enemy and an alien. *"Then the eyes of both of them were opened, and they knew that they were naked; and they sewed fig leaves together and made themselves coverings"* (Genesis 3:7). *"And you . . . were dead in trespasses and sins, in which you once walked according to the course of this world, according to the prince of the power of the air, the spirit who now works in the sons of disobedience, among whom also we all once conducted ourselves in the lusts of our flesh, fulfilling the desires of the flesh and of the mind, and were by nature children of wrath, just as the others"* (Ephesians 2:1-3).

4. If Adam died in his sin, he would suffer eternal punishment for his sin.

How did Adam's sin affect his children?

Adam's sinful nature was passed on to all his posterity. *"Just as through one man sin entered the world, and death through sin, and thus death spread to all men, because all sinned"* (Romans 5:12; see vv. 13-19).

Do you mean that we are all born into the world as sinners because of Adam's sin?

Yes! Adam could only pass on his own nature, and that nature was sinful. All children have to be taught to do right, but they know how to do wrong without being taught. King David wrote, *"Behold, I was brought forth in iniquity, and in sin my mother conceived me"* (Psalm 51:5). As an illustration, a metal gelatin-mold gives its shape to all the gelatin desserts or salads that are made in it. If you drop the metal pan and it becomes dented, all future desserts made in that mold will show the effects of the fall.

It doesn't seem fair that Adam's sinful nature should be passed down to all of us!

Adam acted as a representative of the human race. Since we are all created as free, moral agents, perhaps we would all eventually have done the same as Adam did anyway. In any case, though we are born sinners, we are often worse than we have to be. Some sins we may feel pulled into; other sins we enjoy and do willingly.

Is there not some good in all human beings?

It depends on whether you are looking at it from God's standpoint or man's. God can find no good in man that would help to earn him a place in heaven. As far as being righteous or qualified for heaven is concerned, God says there is not one. Here is His portrait of a sinner: *"From the sole of the foot even to the head, there is no soundness in it, but wounds and bruises and putrefying sores; they have not been closed or bound up, or soothed with ointment"* (Isaiah 1:6).

Just how bad does God say man is?

In short, man is totally depraved, meaning that sin has affected every part of a man's being, and that although he might not have committed every sin, he is capable of doing so. *"The heart is deceitful above all things, and desperately wicked; who can know it?"* (Jeremiah 17:9). *"As it is written: 'There is none righteous, no, not one; there is none who understands; there is none who seeks after God. They have all turned aside; they have together become unprofitable; there is none who does good, no, not one'"* (Romans 3:10-12). *"For I know that in me (that is, in my flesh) nothing good dwells; for to will is present with me, but how to perform what is good I do not find"* (Romans 7:18). In addition, to be totally depraved means that the human race is totally incapable of pleasing God, as far as salvation is concerned. *"So then, those who are in the flesh cannot please God"* (Romans 8:8).

But will God find fault with a person who has not committed the terrible sins of murder, drunkenness, immorality, and so forth?

God sees not only what a person has done, but also what he is in himself. What a man is, is a lot worse than anything he has ever done. A filthy thought life, a hatred of some other person, a lustful look—these are terrible sins in God's sight. *"You have heard that it was said to those of old, 'You shall not commit adultery.' But I say to you that whoever looks at a woman to lust for her has already committed adultery with her in his heart"* (Matthew 5:27-28). *"For from within, out of the heart of men, proceed evil thoughts, adulteries, fornications, murders, thefts, covetousness, wickedness, deceit, lewdness, an evil eye, blasphemy, pride, foolishness. All these evil things come from within and defile a man"* (Mark 7:21-23). *"Because the carnal mind is enmity against God for it is not subject to the law of God, nor indeed can be. So then, those who are in the flesh cannot please God"* (Romans 8:7-8). Sin separates man from God. *"Behold, the LORD's hand is not shortened, that it cannot save; nor His ear heavy, that it cannot hear. But your iniquities have separated you from your God; and your sins have hidden His face from you, so that He will not hear"* (Isaiah 59:1-2).

But are not some sinners worse than others?

Undoubtedly they are, but we must not compare ourselves with others. The Bible states that people who do are not wise. We will not be judged in comparison with others but in light of God's holiness and perfection. *"Therefore you are inexcusable, O man, whoever you are who judge, for in whatever you judge another you condemn yourself, for you who judge practice the same things. But we know that the judgment of God is according to truth against those who practice such things. And do you think this, O man, you who judge those practicing such things, and doing the same, that you will escape the judgment of God?"* (Romans 2:1-3). *"For we dare not class ourselves or compare ourselves with those who commend themselves. But they, measuring themselves by themselves, and comparing themselves among themselves, are not wise"* (2 Corinthians 10:12).

Will all sinners suffer the same punishment?

No! All who die in their sins will spend eternity in the lake of fire. However, there will be degrees of punishment, depending on the opportunities a person has had to be saved and the sins he has committed. We read that when Jesus began to rebuke the unrepentant cities where most of His miracles had been done, He said: *"Woe to you, Chorazin! Woe to you, Bethsaida! For if the mighty works which were done in you had been done in Tyre and Sidon, they would have repented long ago in sackcloth and ashes. But I say to you, it will be more tolerable for Tyre and Sidon in the day of judgment than for you"* (Matthew 11:21-22). Tyre and Sidon had been given some opportunities; Chorazin and Bethsaida had been given more; but they all had squandered the opportunities they were given.

What about those who never hear the gospel?

God has revealed Himself to all mankind in creation as well as in conscience. If a heathen lives up to this knowledge, God will send him further light so that he might be saved. But the heathen has rejected the knowledge of the true God and has worshiped idols of wood and stone. Therefore, he is without excuse: *"For since the creation of the world His invisible attributes are clearly seen, being understood by the things that are made, even His eternal power and Godhead, so that they are without excuse"* (Romans 1:20). Without Christ as Savior, the heathen is lost, and that is why Christians must go into all the world with the gospel.

How could you prove to me that I am a sinner?

If you have never trusted Christ as your Lord and Savior, then you are lost and you need to be saved. If you have to answer "No" to any of the following questions, this is clear proof that you are a sinner.

Your Answer
Yes or *No*

1. Do you love God with all your heart, soul, strength, and mind? _____

2. Do you love your neighbor as you love yourself? _____

3. Would you like your friends to know the most impure thought you have ever had? _____

4. Have you always performed all the good you knew you should do? _____

6. Can you honestly say that you have never used the name of God or Jesus as a curse word? _____

7. Have you an unbroken record of never having told a lie? _____

8. Are you as perfect as the Lord Jesus Christ? _____

The Necessity of Salvation

What is God's attitude toward sin?

Because God is absolutely holy, He cannot approve or excuse sin. Because He is absolutely just, He must punish sin wherever He finds it. He has decreed that *"the wages of sin is death"* (Romans 6:23).

What is God's attitude toward sinners?

God loves the people whom He has made. While He does not love sin, yet He does love the sinner. *"But God demonstrates His own love toward us, in that while we were still sinners, Christ died for us"* (Romans 5:8).

What is God's desire for all sinners?

God's desire for all is that they be saved. He does not want them to perish. *"The Lord is not slack [slow] concerning His promise, as some count slackness, but is longsuffering toward us, not willing that any should perish but that all should come to repentance"* (2 Peter 3:9).

What problem was raised by the entrance of sin into the world?

It raised the problem as to how God could save ungodly sinners and still be righteous in doing so. He wanted *". . . to demonstrate at the present time His righteousness, that He might be just and the justifier of the one who has faith in Jesus"* (Romans 3:26).

Why was this a problem?

God's love desired the salvation of sinners. *"Say to them: 'As I live,' says the LORD God, 'I have no pleasure in the death of the wicked, but that the wicked turn from his way and live. Turn, turn from your evil ways! For why should you die, O house of Israel?'"* (Ezekiel 33:11). Yet because of His holiness, He could not permit sinful creatures to enter His heaven. *"Do you not know that the unrighteous will not inherit the kingdom of God? Do not be deceived. Neither fornicators, nor idolaters, nor adulterers, nor homosexuals, nor sodomites, nor thieves, nor covetous, nor drunkards, nor revilers, nor extortioners will inherit the kingdom of God"* (1 Corinthians 6:9-10). In fact, His justice demanded that all sinners must die as a result of their sins. *"As it is appointed for men to die once, but after this the judgment"* (Hebrews 9:27). The problem, then, was this: how could God's love be satisfied without violating His holiness and His justice?

What would have happened if God had done nothing?

All sinners would have perished in hell. *"The wicked shall be turned into hell, and all the nations that forget God"* (Psalm 9:17).

Isn't God too good to send men to hell?

God is good but He is also righteous and holy. Not one of His attributes (character traits) can triumph at the expense of another. His love can only be exercised in a righteous, holy way.

Would God have been right if He had done nothing?

Yes. Then we all would have received exactly what we deserved. But God's love impelled Him to action.

How could God solve this problem?

He could solve it only by finding a substitute to die in the place of guilty sinners.

What requirements would such a substitute have to meet?

First of all, he would have to be a man; otherwise the substitution would not be a fair one. Then he must be a sinless man. If he were not sinless, he would have to die for his own sins. Third, he must be God, since the Substitute must be able to put away all the sins of all the sinful people in human history. Finally, he must be willing to die for sinners; otherwise Satan would charge God with unjustly making an innocent victim die unwillingly for guilty rebels.

Could such a substitute be found?

Yes, God found a Substitute who met all these requirements in the Person of His only Son, the Lord Jesus Christ. *"Surely He has borne our griefs and carried our sorrows; yet we esteemed Him stricken, smitten by God, and afflicted. But He was wounded for our transgressions, He was bruised for our iniquities; the chastisement for our peace was upon Him, and by His stripes we are healed"* (Isaiah 53:4-5).

The Work of Christ

Was Jesus truly man?

Yes, he was born as a baby in Bethlehem, grew up in Nazareth, and ended His ministry at Jerusalem.

Was He sinless?

Yes, he was born of the virgin Mary and so did not inherit Adam's sin. He knew no sin; he did no sin; there was no sin in Him. *"For He [God] made Him [Christ] who knew no sin to be sin for us, that we might become the righteousness of God in Him"* (2 Corinthians 5:21). *"Who committed no sin, nor was deceit found in His mouth"* (1 Peter 2:22). *"And you know that He was man manifested to take away our sins, and in Him there is no sin"* (1 John 3:5).

Is Jesus God?

Yes, Jesus is truly God, just as He is truly man. *"In the beginning was the Word, and the Word was with God, and the Word was God"* (John 1:1). *"Jesus said, 'I and My Father are one'"* (John 10:30). *"For in Him dwells all the fullness of the Godhead bodily"* (Colossians 2:9).

Speaking of God's special recognition of the Lord Jesus, we read, *"But to the Son He says: 'Your throne, O God, is forever and ever; a scepter of righteousness is the scepter of Your kingdom'"* (Hebrews 1:8).

Was Jesus willing to die as a substitute for sinners?

Yes, He expressed complete willingness to do His Father's will, even if it meant death. The Lord Jesus told His disciples, *"Therefore My Father loves Me, because I lay down My life that I may take it again. No one takes it from Me, but I lay it down of Myself"* (John 10:17-18). *"Then I said, 'Behold, I have come—in the volume of the book it is written of Me to do Your will, O God'"* (Hebrews 10:7).

Couldn't we have been saved by Jesus' sinless life?

No, our sins could never have been put away by His sinless life. Speaking of His own death, Jesus said, *"Most assuredly, I say to you, unless a grain of wheat falls into the ground and dies, it remains alone; but if it dies, it produces much grain"* (John 12:24).

Why did He have to die?

Our sins deserved eternal death. He had to bear the punishment in His body in the way that God had foretold—a tree, a cursed death: *". . . who Himself bore our sins in His own body on the tree, that we, having died to sins, might live for righteousness—by whose stripes you were healed"* (1 Peter 2:24).

Was there any special requirement for the death of the substitute?

Yes, His blood must be shed. Our salvation could not be purchased with money, *"but with the precious blood of Christ . . ."* (1 Peter 1:19).

Why was this necessary?

God had decreed that *"according to the law almost all things are purified with blood, and without shedding of blood there is no remission"* (Hebrews 9:22).

What is the importance of the blood?

The blood is the life of the flesh. The shedding of Christ's blood indicated the giving of His life as a Substitute for sinners. *"For the life of the flesh is in the blood, and I have given it to you upon the altar to make atonement for your souls; for it is the blood that makes atonement for the soul"* (Leviticus 17:11).

What actually happened on the cross?

In the three hours of darkness, God caused all our sins to be placed on the Lord Jesus. In those three hours He endured the eternal death which those sins deserved. *"All we like sheep have gone astray; we have turned, every one, to his own way; and the Lord has laid on Him the iniquity of us all"* (Isaiah 53:6).

Did Jesus say anything from the cross?

Jesus is recorded making seven statements from the cross. One of the last things He said was, *"It is finished!"* (John 19:30).

What did He mean by this?

He meant that the work paying for our sin had been completed; that everything necessary for the salvation of sinners had been provided. *"For by one offering He has perfected forever those who are being sanctified"* (Hebrews 10:14).

What happened to Jesus after His death?

His body was buried in a tomb, but on the third day God raised Him from among the dead. Here are the events described by Luke, Jesus' third biographer: *"Now on the first day of the week, very early in the morning, they and certain other women with them, came to the tomb bringing the spices which they had prepared. But they found the stone rolled away from the tomb. Then they went in and did not find the body of the Lord Jesus. And it happened, as they were greatly perplexed about this, that behold, two men stood by them in shining garments. Then, as they were afraid and bowed their faces to the earth, they said to them, 'Why do you seek the living among the dead? He is not here, but is risen! Remember how he spoke to you when He was still in Galilee, saying, "The Son of Man must be delivered into the hands of sinful men, and be crucified, and the third day rise again"'"* (Luke 24:1-7).

John adds, *"So there they laid Jesus, because of the Jews' Preparation Day, for the tomb was nearby"* (John 19:42).

Why was the resurrection necessary?

By raising Him from the dead, God indicated His complete satisfaction with the work of His Son, *"who was delivered up because of our offenses, and was raised because of our justification"* (Romans 4:25).

Did Jesus rise from the dead in a literal body?

Yes, His body was a real body of flesh and bones. *"Behold My hands and My feet, that it is I Myself,"* He said. *"Handle Me and see, for a spirit does not have flesh and bones as you see I have"* (Luke 24:39).

Could sinful people be saved apart from the resurrection?

No, the resurrection was absolutely necessary for the salvation of human beings. The apostle Paul wrote: *"And if Christ is not risen, then our preaching is empty and your faith is also empty. Yes, and we are found false witnesses of God, because we have testified of God that He raised up Christ, whom he did not raise up-if in fact the dead do not rise. For if the dead do not rise, then Christ is not risen. And if Christ is not risen, your faith is futile; you are still in your sins! Then also those who have fallen asleep in Christ have perished. If in this life only we have hope in Christ, we are of all men the most pitiable"* (1 Corinthians 15:14-19).

What happened after the resurrection?

Forty days later, the Savior went back into heaven where He was honored and glorified by God the Father. The ascension is described in these words, *"Now when He [Jesus] had spoken these things, while they watched, He was taken up, and a cloud received Him out of their sight"* (Acts 1:9).

Who produces conviction of sin in a person's life and shows him his need for a Savior?

The Holy Spirit of God is the One who produces conviction of sin. When the Lord Jesus went back to heaven, He asked the Father to send the Holy Spirit to earth to announce the wonderful news that a way had been provided by which guilty sinners could be saved. The Lord Jesus had described this special work just before He went to die on the cross: *"Nevertheless I tell you the truth. It is to your advantage that I go away; for if I do not go away, the Helper will not come to you; but if I depart, I will send Him to you. And when He has come, He will convict the world of sin, and of righteousness, and of judgment: of sin, because they do not believe in Me; of righteousness, because I go to My Father and you see Me no more; of judgment, because the ruler of this world is judged"* (John 16:7-11).

The Way of Salvation

Since Christ has finished the work of redemption, then are not all people saved?

No, Christ's work is *sufficient* in its scope and power to save all men, but it is *effective* only for those who are willing to receive Him. This may be illustrated by an incident from American history. In 1830, George Wilson was tried by a United States court in Philadelphia for robbery and murder, and sentenced to be hanged. Andrew Jackson, President of the United States, pardoned him. But Wilson refused the pardon, and insisted that it was not a pardon unless he accepted it. The question was brought before the Supreme Court, and Chief Justice John Marshall wrote the following decision: "A pardon is a paper, the value of which depends upon its acceptance by the person implicated. It is hardly to be supposed that one under sentence of death would refuse to accept a pardon, but if it is refused, it is no pardon. George Wilson must hang." And he was hanged.

Why doesn't God save everyone?

He desires to do so, for the Bible says clearly that God *"desires all men to be saved and to come to the knowledge of the truth"* (1 Timothy 2:4). However, He has chosen to give men their choice in the matter of salvation. Otherwise He would take men to heaven who didn't want to be there, and for such it would scarcely be heaven.

What must happen to a person before he can go to heaven?

His sins must be put away and he must be given a new nature that enables him to enjoy heaven. In John chapter 3, we have the record of a conversation between a highly respected religious leader and the Lord Jesus. At one point, Jesus answered and said to him, *"Most assuredly, I say to you, unless one is born again, he cannot see the kingdom of God"* (John 3:3). He also said, *"Most assuredly, I say to you, unless one is born of water and the Spirit, he cannot enter the kingdom of God"* (John 3:5).

How is a person saved?

"By grace you are saved through faith, and that not of yourselves; it is the gift of God, not of works, lest anyone should boast" (Ephesians 2:8-9).

What is meant by grace?

Grace is the unmerited favor of God shown to people who deserve the very opposite. It is God offering salvation to sinners as a free gift. *"But God demonstrates His own love toward us, in that while we were still sinners, Christ died for us"* (Romans 5:8), *". . . that in the ages to come He might show the exceeding riches of His grace in His kindness toward us in Christ Jesus"* (Ephesians 2:7).

What is faith?

Faith is complete belief or trust. By taking God at His word, a person receives salvation from Him as a free gift.

What must a person believe to be saved?

He must believe on the Lord Jesus Christ. *"For God so loved the world that He gave His only begotten Son, that whoever believes in Him should not perish but have everlasting life"* (John 3:16). *"And truly Jesus did many other signs in the presence of His disciples, which are not written in this book; but these are written that you may believe that Jesus is the Christ, the Son of God, and that believing you may have life in His name"* (John 20:30-31).

Is it not enough to believe that there is a God?

No, even the devils believe that, and tremble, but they are not saved. *"You believe that there is one God. You do well. Even the demons believe, and tremble!"* (James 2:19).

What does it mean to believe on Jesus?

It means to confess that you are a sinner needing salvation and to receive Him as your only hope of salvation, acknowledging Him to be Lord of your life. *"If you confess with your mouth the Lord Jesus and believe in your heart that God has raised Him from the dead, you will be saved"* (Romans 10:9).

Is it not enough to believe all the historical facts about Jesus?

No, a person may believe all that the Bible says about Jesus and still be lost. Obviously the people who crucified Jesus knew the historical facts about Him, yet they still rejected Him.

What else is necessary then?

True belief involves a commitment of one's entire self to Jesus as their only Lord and Savior.

Can a person have faith and not be saved?

Certainly! Everyone is a believer in something. Faith in an unworthy object will only bring disappointment. Our faith must be in Christ if we are to be saved.

Can anyone do this?

Salvation is offered to all, but it is only those who admit themselves to be lost who will ever want to be saved. *"For the Son of Man has come to seek and to save that which was lost"* (Luke 19:10).

What can a person do who does not realize he is a sinner?

He should read the Bible and be honest with himself and with God. *"So then faith comes by hearing, and hearing by the word of God"* (Romans 10:17).

What will happen then?

The Holy Spirit of God will show this person that he is a sinner, and that if he dies as he is he will go to hell. Jesus said these solemn words to some who refused to believe on Him: *"I am going away, and you will seek Me, and will die in your sin. Where I go you cannot come . . . Therefore I said to you that you will die in your sins; for if you do not believe that I am He, you will die in your sins"* (John 8:21, 24).

Will a person be saved by seeing this?

No, he must then repent of his sins and receive the Lord Jesus Christ as His Savior. *"He who covers his sins will not prosper, but whoever confesses and forsakes them will have mercy"* (Proverbs 28:13). *"Believe on the Lord Jesus Christ, and you will be saved"* (Acts 16:31).

To be saved simply through faith seems too easy, doesn't it?

It might seem too easy, but it is God's only way of salvation. While it may seem easy to us, we should remember that it was a very costly transaction for God; it cost Him the death of His only begotten Son. So it is an easy salvation, but not a cheap one. *"'Come now, and let us reason together,' says the LORD, 'Though your sins are like scarlet, they shall be as white as snow; though they are red like crimson, they shall be as wool'"* (Isaiah 1:18).

Why did God decide that salvation should be given on the basis of faith?

The reason is that believing on Him is the only thing that anyone can do. Even a child can believe. The gospel was designed so that all may come to Him. *"And let him who hears say, 'Come!' And let him who thirsts come. Whoever desires, let him take the water of life freely"* (Revelation 22:17).

But isn't there some kind of work a person must *do* in order to be saved?

No, there is no work a person can do. Christ finished the work on Calvary's cross. All the sinner has to do is believe. Salvation is *"not by works of righteousness which we have done, but according to His mercy He saved us, through the washing of regeneration and renewing of the Holy Spirit"* (Titus 3:5).

Isn't that a contradiction? You say there is nothing to *do*. *All* you have to *do* is believe.

There is nothing you can do by way of earning or meriting God's approval. There is nothing you can do to buy your way or help purchase your admission to heaven. *"Now to him who works, the wages are not counted as grace but as debt. But to him who does not work but believes on Him who justifies the ungodly, his faith is accounted for righteousness"* (Romans 4:4-5). Faith is a non-meritorious act. When some asked Jesus what they could do to *"work the works of God,"* He said to believe on Him (John 6:28-29). A person cannot be proud because he believes in the Lord; what is more reasonable than for a man to trust his Creator? Thus, faith excludes human boasting and is the only thing a person can do without doing a "good work" that He might think would entitle him to heaven. *"Where is boasting then? It is excluded. By what law? Of works? No, but by the law of faith"* (Romans 3:27).

You're saying that we are not saved by good works?

That is what the Bible says: *". . . not of works, lest anyone should boast"* (Ephesians 2:9).

Why couldn't we be saved by doing good works?

We are sinners and everything we do is stained by sin. The best we can do is like filthy rags in God's sight. *"But we are all like an unclean thing, and all our righteousnesses are like filthy rags"* (Isaiah 64:6).

But suppose I could live a perfect life from this day forward, would I not be saved?

No, you would not, because God requires that which is past. Your past sins must somehow be put away before you could enter God's presence. *"That which is has already been, and what is to be has already been; and God requires an account of what is past"* (Ecclesiastes 3:15).

You mean to say that decent, self-respecting, cultured people don't go to heaven?

The only people who go to heaven are those who acknowledge themselves to be sinners and who confess Jesus Christ as Lord and Savior. Speaking to Jewish religious leaders, *"Jesus said to them, 'Assuredly, I say to you that tax collectors and harlots enter the kingdom of God before you'"* (Matthew 21:31).

Aren't there some people who are not good enough for heaven and not bad enough for hell?

No, there are only two classes of people—saved and unsaved. *"For the message of the cross is foolishness to those who are perishing, but to us who are being saved it is the power of God"* (1 Corinthians 1:18).

Well, then, are there not some people who are too wicked to be saved?

No, the gospel invitation is extended to all mankind, and whoever wants to come may do so. *"Let the wicked forsake his way, and the unrighteous man his thoughts; let him return to the LORD, and He will have mercy on him; and to our God, for He will abundantly pardon"* (Isaiah 55:7). The apostle Paul said, *"This is a faithful saying and worthy of all acceptance, that Christ Jesus came into the world to save sinners, of whom I am chief"* (1 Timothy 1:15). *"Therefore He is also able to save to the uttermost those who come to God through Him, since He always lives to make intercession for them"* (Hebrews 7:25).

Doesn't a person have to clean up his life before he can be saved?

As long as he thinks he can clean up his own life, he won't feel the need of a Savior. He should simply come to Christ just as he is, sins and all, and receive pardon and peace. *"'Come now, and let us reason together,' says the LORD, 'though your sins are like scarlet, they shall be as white as snow; though they are red like crimson, they shall be as wool'"*(Isaiah 1:18). *"But go and learn what this means: 'I desire mercy and not sacrifice'. For I did not come to call the righteous, but sinners, to repentance"* (Matthew 9:13). *"For the Son of Man has come to seek and to save that which was lost"* (Luke 19:10).

Couldn't I be saved by following Jesus' example?

Jesus' life was sinless. No mere man is able to follow that example. Moreover, the only reason Jesus died is because men could be saved in no other way. *"Who Himself bore our sins in His own body on the tree, that we, having died to sins, might live for righteousness—by whose stripes you were healed"* (1 Peter 2:24).

If believing on Jesus is the right way, why do the majority of people refuse to accept Him?

The Bible says that Satan has "blinded" the minds of those *"who do not believe, lest the light of the gospel of the glory of Christ, who is the image of God, should shine on them"* (2 Corinthians 4:4). Also, many think they know better than what the Word of God says: *"There is a way that seems right to a man, but its end is the way of death"* (Proverbs 14:12).

Couldn't a person be saved by trying to keep "the Golden Rule"?

No. When Jesus said, *"whatsoever ye would that men should do to you, do ye even so to them"* (Matthew 7:12, KJV), He never intended it as the way to heaven, because no man can keep the Golden Rule perfectly.

Are you telling me that a person cannot be saved by keeping the Ten Commandments?

No one can fulfill what is demanded by the Ten Commandments. *"Therefore by the deeds of the law no flesh will be justified in His sight, for by the law is the knowledge of sin"* (Romans 3:20).

Exactly what do the Ten Commandments require?

The Ten Commandments (see Exodus 20:1-17) are as follows:

1. You shall have no other god before Me (God).
2. You shall not make for yourself a carved image, etc.
3. You shall not take the name of the Lord your God in vain.
4. Remember the Sabbath day, to keep it holy.
5. Honor your father and your mother.
6. You shall not murder.
7. You shall not commit adultery.
8. You shall not steal.
9. You shall not bear false witness against your neighbor.
10. You shall not covet.

Weren't the commandments given by God to His people?

Yes, they were, but He never intended that they should serve as a means of salvation. *"Knowing that a man is not justified by the works of the law but by faith in Jesus Christ, even we have believed in Christ Jesus, that we might be justified by faith in Christ and not by the works of the law; for by the works of the law no flesh shall be justified"* (Galatians 2:16). *"But that no one is justified by the law in the sight of God is evident, for 'the just shall live by faith'"* (Galatians 3:11).

Then why did God give the commandments?

They were given to show the people what sinners they were. Just as a straight line shows up a crooked line, so the law shows men how far they have departed from God's standard of perfection. *"Moreover the law entered that the offense might abound. But where sin abounded, grace abounded much more"* (Romans 5:20). *"What purpose then does the law serve? It was added because of transgressions, till the Seed should come to whom the promise was made; and it was appointed through angels by the hand of a mediator"* (Galatians 3:19).

Has anyone ever kept these laws perfectly?

The Lord Jesus Christ is the only One who has ever kept the law perfectly. *"For such a High Priest was fitting for us, who is holy, harmless, undefiled, separate from sinners, and has become higher than the heavens"* (Hebrews 7:26).

Then are we not saved through His keeping of the law?

No, we are only saved through His death, burial, and resurrection. We are condemned and cursed by the law. The apostle Paul wrote: *"I do not set aside the grace of God; for if righteousness comes through the law, then Christ died in vain"* (Galatians 2:21).

If a man could keep the law all his life, would he be saved by this?

Such a man would need to have been born a perfect being. But the Bible states: *"If we say that we have not sinned, we make Him [God] a liar, and His word is not in us"* (1 John 1:10).

Suppose that a man could keep nine of the Ten Commandments—would he be saved?

No, the law demands continual and complete obedience. If a person breaks one commandment, he is guilty of breaking all the law. *"For whoever shall keep the whole law, and yet stumble in one point, he is guilty of all"* (James 2:10).

What is the penalty for failing to keep the law?

Death, now and forever. *"For as many as are of the works of the law are under the curse, for it is written, 'Cursed is everyone who does not continue in all things which are written in the book of the law, to do them'"* (Galatians 3:10).

Weren't the Ten Commandments made for good people?

No! *"The law is not made for a righteous person, but for the lawless and insubordinate, for the ungodly and for sinners, for the unholy and profane, for murderers of fathers and murderers of mothers, for manslayers, for fornicators, for sodomites, for kidnappers, for liars, for perjurers, and if there is any other thing that is contrary to sound doctrine"* (1 Timothy 1:9-10).

What effect should the commandments have on us?

They should make us realize what guilty sinners we are, and should cause us to cast ourselves on the mercy of the Lord. *"Now we know that whatever the law says, it says to those who are under the law, that every mouth may be stopped, and all the world may become guilty before God"* (Romans 3:19).

But does it seem reasonable that we should be saved by faith alone and not by faith plus good works?

The Scripture says, *"Not by works of righteousness which we have done, but according to His mercy He saved us . . ."* (Titus 3:5).

Doesn't it say somewhere in the Bible that "faith without works is dead"?

Yes, it says that in James 2:20. The teaching of the passage is that a man may say that he has faith but if he does not have good works, it shows that he was never truly saved. That kind of a faith never saved anyone.

What kind of a faith *does* save?

The kind that is not merely a matter of the lips but of the heart, which results in a new life filled with good works.

Then you mean that good works follow salvation, but do not secure it?

Yes, that is right. We are not saved *by* good works, but we are saved *unto* good works. *"For by grace you have been saved through faith, and that not of yourselves; it is the gift of God, not of works, lest anyone should boast. For we are His workmanship, created in Christ Jesus for good works, which God prepared beforehand that we should walk in them"* (Ephesians 2:8-10).

Does God expect us to join a church?

Whenever a person is saved, he becomes a member of the true church composed of all true believers in the Lord Jesus. Then he should find fellowship in a local church where Christ is acknowledged as Head and where the Bible is accepted as the only inspired Word of God, our sufficient guide in all matters of faith and morals.

Doesn't the fact that I was baptized as an infant mean that I am saved?

Baptism is not the Savior. Only Jesus Christ can save. *"Jesus said to him, 'I am the way, the truth, and the life. No one comes to the Father except through Me'"* (John 14:6).

But shouldn't people be baptized?

Those who have been born again (saved) should be baptized. However, there is no clear record in the New Testament of unsaved people or infants ever being baptized.

Then I am not saved by partaking of the communion service either?

No. Once again, the communion service was only intended for those who are already born again believers in the Lord Jesus Christ.

Are you saying that church attendance, charity, participating in the ordinances, and other observances will not help in my salvation?

They will not help at all in the matter of your salvation. The only thing that will help you is to come to Christ as a sinner, repent of your sins, and trust Him as your only hope for heaven. *"Neither is there salvation in any other, for there is no other name under heaven given among men by which we must be saved"* (Acts 4:12).

General Difficulties

How do I know that the Lord will accept me if I believe on Him?

He has said that He will, and He cannot lie. *"The one who comes to Me I will by no means cast out"* (John 6:37). *"Whoever calls on the name of the Lord shall be saved"* (Acts 2:21).

But doesn't it seem like a leap in the dark, this business of believing?

No, it is the surest thing in the world. Banks may fail, businesses may go bankrupt, governments may topple, and men may break their promises. But God cannot go back on His word. He has promised to save all who receive Christ by faith. *"He who believes in Him is not condemned, but he who does not believe is condemned already, because he has not believed in the name of the only begotten Son of God"* (John 3:18). God makes a genuine offer of salvation to any person in the world who will receive Christ Jesus as Lord. You can be saved if you will do what God says. *"He who believes in the Son has everlasting life; and he who does not believe the Son shall not see life, but the wrath of God abides on him"* (John 3:36).

I would like to be saved, but I'm afraid that I wouldn't be able to hold out.

No one has the strength in himself to hold out. However, when God saves you, He gives you strength you never had before. Every believer has the Holy Spirit of God living within him. It is from the Holy Spirit that the child of God receives power to live the Christian life. *"For as many as are led by the Spirit of God, these are sons of God"* (Romans 8:14). We *"are kept by the power of God"* (1 Peter 1:5).

Suppose I have committed the unpardonable sin?

The unpardonable sin, according to the Lord Jesus, was saying that the miracles He performed were done not by the power of the Holy Spirit but by the power of the devil. Have you ever said this? If not, then you have not committed the unpardonable sin. *"Every sin and blasphemy will be forgiven men, but the blasphemy against the Spirit will not be forgiven men. Anyone who speaks a word against the Son of Man, it will be forgiven him; but whoever speaks against the Holy Spirit, it will not be forgiven him, either in this age or in the age to come"* (Matthew 12:31-32).

But if you die rejecting Christ, you will have committed an equally serious sin for which there is no forgiveness. *"For what will it profit a man if he gains the whole world, and loses his own soul? Or what will a man give in exchange for his soul?"* (Mark 8:36-37).

But trusting Christ means that I will have to give up a lot, doesn't it?

Christ does not come to rob us but to enrich us. He said, *"I have come that they may have life, and that they may have it more abundantly"* (John 10:10). An unbelieving sailor once said to his Christian friend, "I just can't face the cost of becoming a Christian." The friend replied, "Have you ever faced the cost of *not* becoming a Christian?"

But there are so many hypocrites in the church.

Don't despise those who are real just because some are hypocrites. Determine instead that *you* will be a true follower of the Lord.

Sometimes I think I have believed in the Lord Jesus, but how do I know I have believed in the right way?

If you have no other hope for heaven apart from Jesus Christ, if you have repented of your sins, if you made a complete commitment of yourself to Him, then you have believed in the right way. It is not how much you believe but the Person in whom you trust. *"For I know whom I have believed and am persuaded that He is able to keep what I have committed to Him until that Day"* (2 Timothy 1:12).

Would it not be all right for me to postpone any decision about salvation until I am near the end of my life?

Four Scriptures answer this question. *"Do not boast about tomorrow, for you do not know what a day may bring forth"* (Proverbs 27:1). *"He who is often rebuked, and hardens his neck, will suddenly be destroyed, and that without remedy"* (Proverbs 29:1). *"Remember now your Creator in the days of your youth, before the difficult days come, and the years draw near when you say, 'I have no pleasure in them'"* (Ecclesiastes 12:1). *"Behold, now is the accepted time; behold, now is the day of salvation"* (2 Corinthians 6:2b).

Is there no other way I can come to God except through Jesus?

There is no other way. Jesus said, *"I am the way, the truth, and the life. No one comes to the Father except through Me"* (John 14:6). *"For there is one God and one Mediator between God and men, the Man Christ Jesus, who gave Himself a ransom for all, to be testified in due time"* (1 Timothy 2:5-6).

Relationship and Fellowship

Do Christians still sin?

Yes, Christians sin every day—in thought, word, and actions. They are guilty of sins of omission as well as sins of commission. As the apostle Paul described his own struggle: *"The good that I will to do, I do not do; but the evil I will not to do, that I practice"* (Romans 7:19).

Should Christians sin?

No, God's will is that Christians should not sin. The apostle John wrote: *"My little children, these things I write to you, so that you may not sin. And if anyone sins, we have an Advocate with the Father, Jesus Christ the righteous"* (1 John 2:1).

When a Christian sins, does he lose his salvation?

No, salvation is the free gift of God, and, once it is given, it is never taken back again. The Lord Jesus said, *"My sheep hear My voice, and I know them, and they follow Me. And I give them eternal life, and they shall never perish; neither shall anyone snatch them out of My hand. My Father, who has given them to Me, is greater than all; and no one is able to snatch them out of My Father's hand"* (John 10:27-29).

But doesn't the penalty of those sins have to be paid?

Jesus Christ bore the penalty of those sins when He died on the cross of Calvary. God does not require the penalty to be paid twice.

You mean, then, that a Christian is still a child of God, even though he sins?

Yes, his relationship in the family of God is eternal. When a son is born into a human family, he will always be a son of his parents. He may disgrace them by his behavior, but he is still their son. So it is in the family of God; relationship is established by the new birth and nothing can ever change it. *"But as many as received Him, to them He gave the right to become children of God, to those who believe in His name"* (John 1:12).

What does happen, then, when a Christian sins?

One thing that happens is that fellowship with the Lord is broken. *"If we say that we have fellowship with Him, and walk in darkness, we lie and do not practice the truth"* (1 John 1:6).

What is fellowship?

Fellowship is the happy family spirit that results from all the members having the same interests and sharing things in common. Consider the following illustration. A judge in the criminal court finds a robber guilty and sentences him to twelve months in jail. When the judge goes home that night, he finds that his little boy has been naughty. But does he sentence him to twelve months in jail? No, he no longer acts as a judge, but as a father in a family. The child is still his son, even though naughty. Because of sin, the happy family spirit has been broken and it remains broken until that sin has been confessed and forgiven. So the child is probably sent upstairs and he remains there until he is willing to confess his wrong. The great point is that *relationship* is not affected, but *fellowship* is. When a person is a sinner, God is his Judge; but when that person becomes saved, God from then on is his Father.

Then you mean to say that once a person is saved he can never be lost?

That is what the Bible says. *"They shall never perish"* (John 10:28). *"He who hears My word and believes in Him who sent Me has everlasting life, and shall not come into judgment, but has passed from death into life"* (John 5:24). *"I am persuaded that neither death nor life, nor angels nor principalities nor powers, nor things present nor things to come, nor height nor depth, nor any other created thing, shall be able to separate us from the love of God which is in Christ Jesus our Lord"* (Romans 8:38-39). *"Now to Him who is able to keep you from stumbling, and to present you faultless before the presence of His glory with exceeding joy, to God our Savior, who alone is wise, be glory and majesty, dominion and power, both now and forever. Amen"* (Jude 1:24-25).

Can a person decide to be saved and later change his mind?

When a person has once committed his life to the Lord Jesus Christ, then his eternal salvation becomes the sole responsibility of the Savior. *"This is the will of the Father who sent Me, that of all He has given Me I should lose nothing, but should raise it up at the last day"* (John 6:39). The Lord is honor-bound to take that person home to heaven. And because the Holy Spirit dwells in the true believer, he never will change his mind about being saved.

Does that mean that a Christian can sin all he wants and still be saved?

A true Christian will not want to sin, because he has a new nature that hates sin. *"Therefore, if anyone is in Christ, he is a new creation; old things have passed away; behold, all things have become new"* (2 Corinthians 5:17).

But suppose a Christian lives in willful and habitual sin?

If a person lives that kind of a life, it indicates that he was never truly born again. *"Whoever has been born of God does not sin, for His seed remains in him; and he cannot sin, because he has been born of God. In this the children of God and the children of the devil are manifest: Whoever does not practice righteousness is not of God, nor is he who does not love his brother"* (1 John 3:9-10).

Can a Christian sin and get away with it?

No, he cannot. While it is true that the legal penalty of his sins has been paid once for all at the cross, it is also true that God administers parental discipline to His erring children. *"Do not be deceived, God is not mocked; for whatever a man sows, that he will also reap. For he who sows to his flesh will of the flesh reap corruption, but he who sows to the Spirit will of the Spirit reap everlasting life"* (Galatians 6:7-8).

How does God discipline His children?

Sometimes it is through sickness or adversity and, in extreme cases, through death itself. Paul wrote about some Christians in the first century, *"For this reason many are weak and sick among you, and many sleep [another word for death]"* (1 Corinthians 11:30).

Does sin in a believer's life have any other consequences in this world?

Yes. He loses his joy. His prayers are hindered. His fruitfulness is marred. His guidance becomes obscure. He suffers shame and remorse. Opportunities are neglected and privileges forfeited. Finally his testimony is ruined. (See David's description in Psalm 51).

Does sin in a believer's life have any eternal consequences?

Yes, he suffers loss at the Judgment Seat of Christ. *"If anyone's work is burned, he will suffer loss; but he himself will be saved, yet so as through fire"* (1 Corinthians 3:15). *"For we must all appear before the judgment seat of Christ, that each one may receive the things done in the body, according to what he has done, whether good or bad"* (2 Corinthians 5:10).

Suppose a Christian dies with unconfessed sin?

As mentioned previously, the penalty for all of a believer's sin was borne by the Lord Jesus. When Christ died, all the Christian's sins were future. Since He paid the complete penalty, we can say He died for the believer's past, present, and future sins. Unconfessed sins, however, will result in a loss of reward at the Judgment Seat of Christ.

Is it possible for a Christian to backslide?

Yes, any child of God may wander away from the Lord.

How may we guard against backsliding?

By reading the Word of God, by spending time in prayer, and by maintaining fellowship with the people of God.

What is the remedy for backsliding?

The cure for backsliding is confession and forsaking of sin, and, if possible, making restitution for wrongs committed.

How to Be Certain of Salvation

If I trust Christ as my Lord and Savior, what will happen inside me to tell me that I am saved?

If you mean some mysterious feeling or emotional experience, then it is quite probable that nothing like that will occur.

How then will I know that I am saved?

In a very simple way. God says He saves those who believe on the Lord Jesus. When you believe on Him, you can know that you are saved because God says so. *"He who believes in the Son of God has the witness in himself, he who does not believe God has made Him a liar, because he has not believed the testimony that God has given of His Son. And this is the testimony: that God has given us eternal life, and this life is in His Son. He who has the Son has life; he who does not have the Son of God does not have life"* (1 John 5:10-12).

You mean I may not feel anything special?

That's right. The real act of salvation takes place in heaven, where the fact is recorded. When God sees your faith, He justifies you (makes you right with Him, acceptable to Him).

But shouldn't a person feel different when he is saved?

Certainly he should, but feelings are not the proof of his salvation. A person will not really feel happy until he knows he is saved. The order is this: salvation through faith in Christ; assurance through the promise of God; joy because of this assurance.

Then a person knows he is saved through the promises of God in the Bible?

That is the first and main way by which he knows he is saved. *"These things I have written to you who believe in the name of the Son of God, that you may know that you have eternal life, and that you may continue to believe in the name of the Son of God"* (1 John 5:13).

So feelings are not a dependable guide?

The trouble with feelings is that they are so changeable. One day a person may feel he is saved and the next he may not. The Word of God never varies. How much better, then, to have our assurance of salvation based on the Word of God!

Is the Bible the only way by which we can know we are saved?

No, there are several others.

1. A love for our fellow Christians. *"We know that we have passed from death to life, because we love the brethren. He who does not love his brother abides in death"* (1 John 3:14).

2. A new love for holiness. *"For I delight in the law of God according to the inward man"* (Romans 7:22).

3. A new hatred of sins. *"O wretched man that I am! Who will deliver me from this body of death?"* (Romans 7:24).

4. Continuing in the faith. *"They went out from us, but they were not of us; for if they had been of us, they would have continued with us; but they went out that they might be made manifest, that none of them were of us"* (1 John 2:19).

5. The witness of the indwelling Holy Spirit. *"For as many as are led by the Spirit of God, these are sons of God"* (Romans 8:14). *"The Spirit Himself bears witness with our spirit that we are children of God"* (Romans 8:16).

May a person be saved and not know it?

It is possible that a person may really have been born again and yet not know it, either because of inadequate teaching or because of doubts placed in his mind by Satan.

May a person think he is saved and yet not be?

Certainly, many think they are saved because of their character or works, but they are not saved at all. *"Many will say to Me in that day, 'Lord, Lord, have we not prophesied in Your name, cast out demons in Your name, and done many wonders in Your name?' And then I will declare to them, 'I never knew you; depart from Me, you who practice lawlessness!'"* (Matthew 7:22-23).

Is it necessary to know the day and hour of one's conversion?

No, it is not. Many people have such a distinct experience that they can tell the exact time and place. Others may not remember when they first trusted the Savior. The important thing is to be able to say, "I know I am saved right now because my faith and trust are in the Lord Jesus Christ alone."

Do most Christians have doubts about their salvation at one time or another?

Most Christians are probably subjected to doubts at some point after their conversion.

What should one do when plagued with doubts?

The best thing to do is to quote Scripture to answer the doubts. When Satan insinuates that the believer is not saved, quote gospel promises like John 5:24, *"Most assuredly, I say to you, he who hears My word and believes in Me who sent Me has everlasting life, and shall not come into judgment, but has passed from death into life."* Just as the Lord used the Word to repel the temptations of Satan, so we should use the Bible to drive away his lies that are designed to make us doubt: *"But He answered and said, 'It is written, "Man shall not live by bread alone, but by every word that proceeds from the mouth of God"'"* (Matthew 4:4). *"Jesus said to him, 'It is written again, "You shall not tempt the Lord your God"'"* (Matthew 4:7). *"Then Jesus said to him, 'Away with you, Satan! For it is written, "You shall worship the Lord your God, and Him only you shall serve"'"* (Matthew 4:10).

If I am not sure whether I have ever really accepted Christ, what should I do?

You should get it settled right now by saying from your heart, "Lord, if I have never trusted You before, I here and now receive You as my only Lord and Savior."

Holiness

Doesn't a person have to live a holy life in order to become a Christian?

No, a sinner is not able to live a holy life until after he is saved.

Does God expect Christians to lead holy lives?

He most certainly does. *"For this is the will of God, your sanctification: that you should abstain from sexual immorality"* (1 Thessalonians 4:3). *"For the grace of God that brings salvation has appeared to all men, teaching us that, denying ungodliness and worldly lusts, we should live soberly, righteously, and godly in the present age, looking for the blessed hope and glorious appearing of our great God and Savior Jesus Christ"* (Titus 2:11-13).

Does any Christian live a life of sinless perfection?

No, no Christian lives a sinless life. *"If we say that we have no sin, we deceive ourselves, and the truth is not in us"* (1 John 1:8). *"If we say that we have not sinned, we make Him a liar, and His word is not in us"* (1 John 1:10). The Lord Jesus Christ is the only Person who ever lived a perfect life.

How is it that Christians can still sin after they are saved?

The reason is that the believer still has the old, evil, corrupt nature with which he was born. This is not removed at the time of conversion. The apostle Paul describes the root of ungodly acts in the believer's life: *"But now, it is no longer I who do it but sin that dwells in me"* (Romans 7:17).

In what way, then, is the believer different from those who are not saved?

The believer has a new nature which he receives at conversion. Scripture speaks of this as the divine nature *"by which have been given to us exceedingly great and precious promises, that through these you may be partakers of the divine nature, having escaped the corruption that is in the world through lust"* (2 Peter 1:4).

What's the difference between the two natures?

The old nature is incurably bad and continually seeks to drag the Christian down into sin. *"Evil is present with me, the one who wills to do good"* (Romans 7:21). The new nature is only capable of good and seeks to lead the believer in holiness. *"For I delight in the law of God according to the inward man"* (Romans 7:22).

Why did God allow the evil nature to remain after conversion?

The old nature teaches us our own nothingness and weakness, and makes us continually dependent on the Lord for strength to resist temptation. *"O wretched man that I am! Who will deliver me from this body of death?"* (Romans 7:24).

Are all Christians tempted to sin?

Yes, all Christians are tempted. *"No temptation has overtaken you except such as is common to man; but God is faithful, who will not allow you to be tempted beyond what you are able, but with the temptation will also make the way of escape, that you may be able to bear it"* (1 Corinthians 10:13).

Does a Christian ever have to yield to temptation?

No, a Christian only sins when he wants to. He has the power of the Holy Spirit living within him, and this power is enough to deliver from all temptation. *"For the flesh lusts against the Spirit, and the Spirit against the flesh; and these are contrary to one another, so that you do not do the things that you wish"* (Galatians 5:17).

What is God's attitude toward the old nature?

God saw that it was worthy of death, so He condemned it at the cross of Calvary. He does not try to reform it, improve it, or clean it up. It is utterly hopeless and so God sees it as having been put to death when Christ died. *"Knowing this, that our old man was crucified with Him, that the body of sin might be done away with, that we should no longer be slaves of sin"* (Romans 6:6).

What should be the believer's attitude toward the old nature?

He should keep it in the place of death—that is, whenever the old nature tries to tell the Christian what to do, he should refuse to obey what has been condemned by God. *"Likewise you also, reckon yourselves to be dead indeed to sin, but alive to God in Christ Jesus our Lord. Therefore do not let sin reign in your mortal body, that you should obey it in its lusts"* (Romans 6:11-12).

What should be the believer's attitude toward the new nature?

He should feed it, cultivate it, and encourage it through studying the Scriptures, spending time in worship and prayer, serving the Lord, and otherwise doing those things that are pleasing to the Lord. *"But the fruit of the Spirit is love, joy, peace, longsuffering, kindness, goodness, faithfulness, gentleness, self-control. Against such there is no law"* (Galatians 5:22-23).

What, in brief, is the secret of living a holy life?

The secret is in being occupied with the Lord Jesus in worship. There is no once-for-all way of achieving holiness; it is a life-long process. Yet the Holy Spirit keeps at it until the transformation is complete: *"But we all, with unveiled face, beholding as in a mirror the glory of the Lord, are being transformed into the same image from glory to glory, just as by the Spirit of the Lord"* (2 Corinthians 3:18).

Can you give other practical helps toward holy living?

1. Guard your thought life; you can control what you think. *"Finally, brethren, whatever things are true, whatever things are noble, whatever things are just, whatever things are pure, whatever things are lovely, whatever things are of good report, if there is any virtue and if there is anything praiseworthy—meditate on these things"* (Philippians 4:8).

2. Make no room for the old nature to operate. *"Put on the Lord Jesus Christ, and make no provision for the flesh, to fulfill its lusts"* (Romans 13:14).

3. Remember that Christ lives within your body. *"To them God willed to make known what are the riches of the glory*

of this mystery among the Gentiles: which is Christ in you, the hope of glory" (Colossians 1:27).

4. In moments of temptation, cry to the Lord to deliver you. *"But when he [Peter] saw that the wind was boisterous, he was afraid; and beginning to sink he cried out, saying, 'Lord, save me!'"* (Matthew 14:30).

5. Keep busy for the Lord. *"Whatever your hand finds to do, do it with your might; for there is no work or device or knowledge or wisdom in the grave where you are going"* (Ecclesiastes 9:10).

6. Engage in some physical exercise. *'For bodily exercise profits a little, but godliness is profitable for all things, having promise of the life that now is and of that which is to come"* (1 Timothy 4:8).

But doesn't the Christian have to keep the Ten Commandments in order to live a holy life?

The Scripture teaches that the believer is not under the Ten Commandments as a rule of life. *"For you are not under law but under grace"* (Romans 6:14).

1. The purpose of the law is to make men realize they are sinners, not to make them holy.

2. The law condemns to death all who do not keep it perfectly. No one can be under the law without being under this curse.

3. Christ paid the penalty of the law which we had broken, and now the law has no claim on the child of God. *"For Christ is the end of the law for righteousness to everyone who believes"* (Romans 10:4). *"Christ has redeemed us*

from the curse of the law, having become a curse for us (for it is written, 'Cursed is everyone who hangs on a tree')" (Galatians 3:13).

4. Nine of the Ten Commandments are repeated in the New Testament. But they are not repeated as law with penalty attached; rather, as instruction in righteousness for the people of God, who are now empowered by the Holy Spirit to live in ways pleasing to God. Sabbath-keeping is the only one that is not repeated.

Does that mean that the Christian can go out and commit murder and adultery?

Not at all. The Christian doesn't want to do these things because of his new life. Men under law live in fear of punishment. Men under grace are constrained by love for Christ. Love is a much stronger motive than fear. Men will do for love what they would never do because of fear.

If the Ten Commandments are not the believer's rule of life, what is?

The life and teachings of Jesus are the pattern and guide for the Christian. *"He who says he abides in Him ought himself also to walk just as He walked"* (1 John 2:6).

How is Jesus' teaching different from the law?

This is answered in the fifth chapter of Matthew. The law said, *"You shall not commit adultery."* Jesus said, *"Whoever looks at a woman to lust for her has already committed adultery with her in his heart"* (see verses 27-28). The law said, *"An eye for an eye and a tooth for a tooth."* Jesus said, *"I tell you not to resist an evil person. But whoever slaps you on your right cheek, turn the other to him also"* (see verses 38-42). The law said, *"Love your neighbor and hate your enemy."* Jesus said, *"Love your enemies"* (see verses 43-44).

Is it possible for men to live as Jesus taught?

Humanly it is impossible. But the Lord has given the Holy Spirit to all believers so that they will have the power to live in this supernatural way. *"Do you not know that your body is the temple of the Holy Spirit who is in you, whom you have from God, and you are not your own?"* (1 Corinthians 6:19). *"I say then: Walk in the Spirit, and you shall not fulfill the lust of the flesh. For the flesh lusts against the Spirit, and the Spirit against the flesh; and these are contrary to one another, so that you do not do the things that you wish"* (Galatians 5:16-17).

"Standing" and "State"

If believers still sin, how can God ever take them to heaven?

All who believe on Christ are given a perfect *standing* before God, even if their *state* may be far from perfect: *"And you are complete in Him [Jesus Christ]"* (Colossians 2:10).

What is meant by a believer's standing?

It means the position of complete favor he has with God because he is in Christ. *"Therefore, having been justified by faith, we have peace with God through our Lord Jesus Christ, through whom also we have access by faith into this grace in which we stand, and rejoice in hope of the glory of God"* (Romans 5:1-2).

The Christian has no right or merit in himself to stand before God. His only title to heaven lies in the Person and work of the Lord Jesus. Thus God accepts us, not because of who or what we are, but because we belong to Christ: *"to the praise of the glory of His grace, by which He made us accepted in the Beloved"* (Ephesians 1:6).

How can God look on unrighteous people as righteous?

He can do it because Christ bore the punishment of their sins in His body on the cross. *"But now in Christ Jesus you who once were far off have been brought near by the blood of Christ"* (Ephesians 2:13).

So God accepts all believers because they come to Him in the Person of His Son?

Yes, that is right. Christ is man's only title to heaven. He Himself said, *"No one comes to the Father except through Me"* (John 14:6).

How long does a believer enjoy this perfect standing before God?

He enjoys it as long as Christ enjoys it, because he is in Christ; He is accepted in the Beloved One. *"In Him you also trusted, after you heard the word of truth, the gospel of your salvation; in whom also, having believed, you were sealed with the Holy Spirit of promise, who is the guarantee of our inheritance until the redemption of the purchased possession, to the praise of His glory"* (Ephesians 1:13-14).

What is meant by the believer's state?

This is his everyday spiritual condition here on earth. Just as his standing is what he is in Christ, so his state is what he is in himself.

Is the believer's state sinless?

No, the believer's state is oftentimes far from being what it should be. *"But now you yourselves are to put off all these: anger, wrath, malice, blasphemy, filthy language out of your mouth. Do not lie to one another, since you have put off the old man with his deeds"* (Colossians 3:8-9).

What is God's will concerning the believer's state?

God's will is that his state should grow more and more like his standing. This is a process that should be taking place continually throughout the Christian life. *"If then you were raised with Christ, seek those things which are above, where Christ is, sitting at the right hand of God"* (Colossians 3:1).

Will a believer's state ever correspond exactly to his standing?

Yes, when Christ takes him home to heaven, his condition will be as perfect as his position. *"Beloved, now we are children of God; and it has not yet been revealed what we shall be, but we know that when He is revealed, we shall be like Him, for we shall see Him as He is"* (1 John 3:2).

Why should a Christian want to have his state correspond increasingly with his standing?

His love for Christ should make him desire this. *"If you love Me, keep My commandments"* (John 14:15), said the Lord.

After Salvation—What?

What is the first thing a person should do after he has trusted Christ?

Common courtesy would suggest that he thank the Lord for saving his soul. When the Lord Jesus met ten lepers one day, He told them, *"'Go, show yourselves to the priests.' And so it was that as they went, they were cleansed. And one of them, when he saw that he was healed, returned, and with a loud voice glorified God, and fell down on his face at His feet, giving Him thanks. And he was a Samaritan. So Jesus answered and said, 'Were there not ten cleansed? But where are the nine? Were there not any found who returned to give glory to God except this foreigner?' And He said to him, 'Arise, go your way. Your faith has made you well'"* (Luke 17:14-19).

Is it necessary to confess Christ to others?

Confession is not necessary to obtain salvation, but it is certainly necessary for growth in the Christian life. No one can ever expect to advance in the things of God who is ashamed of his Savior. *"Whoever confesses Me before men, him I will also confess before My Father who is in heaven. But whoever denies Me before men, him I will also deny before My Father who is in heaven"* (Matthew 10:32-33). *"But sanctify the Lord God in your hearts, and always be ready to give a defense to everyone who asks you a reason for the hope that is in you, with meekness and fear"* (1 Peter 3:15; see also Romans 10:9-10).

How does a person go about confessing Christ?

It is simply a matter of telling others what great things the Lord has done for you. When a man's life was transformed by the Lord Jesus, he asked if he could stay with Him, but Jesus said to him, *"Go home to your friends, and tell them what great things the Lord has done for you, and how He has had compassion on you"* (Mark 5:19).

How long should a new convert wait until he is baptized?

Obedience should be prompt. Baptism is a lovely opportunity to publicly identify oneself with Christ in His death, burial, and resurrection. By this act we are saying that we deserved to die but that Christ died for us. Therefore, when He died, we really died, because He died in our place. We witness that we likewise were buried with Him, and that we rose with Him to walk in newness of life. *"Do you not know that as many of us as were baptized into Christ Jesus were baptized into His death? Therefore we were buried with Him through baptism into death, that just as Christ was raised from the dead by the glory of the Father, even so we also should walk in newness of life"* (Romans 6:3-4).

Does baptism give us merit before God as far as our salvation is concerned?

No, baptism is an act of obedience to the teaching of the Lord Jesus. Those believers who die without being baptized will be unbaptized for all eternity.

How should a young convert know which church to join?

First of all, he should realize that he became a member of the true church, the body of Christ, when he was saved. *"By one Spirit we were all baptized into one body—whether Jews or Greeks, whether slaves or free—and have all been made to drink into one Spirit"* (1 Corinthians 12:13). In addition, he should seek to identify himself with a local church where Christ is acknowledged as Head, where the Bible is accepted as the only guide, where the two ordinances of the church (baptism and the Lord's Supper) are observed, where a good teaching ministry is carried on, and where the gospel is faithfully presented. In associating with Christians, he should feel a deep sense of responsibility to contribute to the welfare of the fellowship by loving service, fervent prayer, and sacrificial giving.

What do you consider the most important things Christians should do each day?

Spend time in the Word of God and in prayer each day, and confess and forsake sin whenever it is allowed into one's life. *"How can a young man cleanse his way? By taking heed according to Your word"* (Psalm 119:9). *"Your word I have hidden in my heart, that I might not sin against You"* (Psalm 119:11).

What does the Lord expect of one who is saved?

He expects a total commitment of that person to Himself. He expects the person to go where He leads, to do what He says, to be what He wants him to be. *"I beseech you therefore, brethren, by the mercies of God, that you present your bodies a living sacrifice, holy, acceptable to God, which is your reasonable service. And do not be conformed to this world, but be transformed by the renewing of your mind, that you may prove what is that good and acceptable and perfect will of God"* (Romans 12:1-2).

Is it reasonable that God should expect this?

Yes, it is the only reasonable response that a person can make to the Lord.

Doesn't a person have to think about himself?

Our chief responsibility in life is to please God. If we seek the kingdom of God and His righteousness, He will see that we have some means of livelihood. *"But seek first the kingdom of God and His righteousness, and all these things [material needs] shall be added to you"* (Matthew 6:33).

Does that mean that I may have to go to the mission field?

It may mean that and it may not. But it does mean that you should be willing to go. *"Then He said to them all, 'If anyone desires to come after Me, let him deny himself, and take up his cross daily, and follow Me. For whoever desires to save his life will lose it, but whoever loses his life for My sake will save it. For what profit is it to a man if he gains the whole world, and is himself destroyed or lost? For whoever is ashamed of Me and My words, of him the Son of Man will be ashamed when He comes in His own glory, and in His Father's, and of the holy angels'"* (Luke 9:23-26).

But I see so many Christians who are enjoying the comforts and luxuries of the world, and who do not seem to be all-out for Christ.

You must not compare yourself with other Christians. Your example is the Lord Jesus, and you must follow His steps. *"Now great multitudes went with Him. And He turned and said to them, 'If anyone comes to Me and does not hate his father and mother, wife and children, brothers and sisters, yes, and his own life also, he cannot be*

My disciple. And whoever does not bear his cross and come after Me cannot be My disciple'" (Luke 14:25-27).

Does Christ really expect us to "hate" our relatives?

He expects our love for Him to be so great that all other loves are hatred by comparison. *"If anyone comes to Me and does not hate his father and mother, wife and children, brothers and sisters, yes, and his own life also, he cannot be My disciple"* (Luke 14:26).

Can I not acknowledge Jesus as my Savior and not as my Lord?

Scripture gives no encouragement to such an attitude. If the Lord Jesus is not worth everything, He is not worth anything.

Then salvation involves a complete surrender to Jesus Christ?

That is exactly right. Nothing short of this will do. As the apostle Paul expressed it, *"I have been crucified with Christ, it is no longer I who live, but Christ lives in me; and the life which I now live in the flesh I live by faith in the Son of God, who loved me and gave Himself for me"* (Galatians 2:20).